Side Dishes

The Taunton Press

ACADEMIA BARILLA
AMBASSADOR OF ITALIAN GASTRONOMY
THROUGHOUT THE WORLD

Academia Barilla is a global movement toward the protection, development and promotion of authentic regional Italian culture and cuisine.
With the concept of Food as Culture at our core, Academia Barilla offers a 360° view of Italy. Our comprehensive approach includes:

- a state-of-the-art culinary center in Parma, Italy;
- gourmet travel programs and hands-on cooking classes;
- the world's largest Italian gastronomic library and historic menu collection;
- a portfolio of premium artisan food products;
- global culinary certification programs;
- custom corporate services and training;
- team building activities;
- and a vast assortment of Italian cookbooks.

Thank you and we look forward to welcoming you in Italy soon!

CONTENTS

EDITED BY
ACADEMIA BARILLA

PHOTOGRAPHS
ALBERTO ROSSI

RECIPES BY
CHEF MARIO GRAZIA
CHEF LUCA ZANGA

TEXT BY
MARIAGRAZIA VILLA

ACADEMIA BARILLA EDITORIAL COORDINATION
CHATO MORANDI
ILARIA ROSSI
REBECCA PICKRELL

GRAPHIC DESIGN
PAOLA PIACCO

As here we shall deal with the cooking of the various sorts of foods, to start with we will begin with those that are the easiest, namely, the vegetables.

LIBER DE COQUINA, (THE BOOK OF COOKING/COOKERY), EARLY 14TH CENTURY

SIDE DISHES

From the very beginning, Italian cuisine has been enamored of vegetables and legumes. It's a long love affair, not a passing fancy. And the *Bel Paese* (the "beautiful country," as Italians call their home) has a variety of agricultural produce worth boasting about, from north to south: red radicchio of Treviso, as lovely to look at as it is delightful to taste; Pachino cherry tomatoes, seemingly invented by some Mediterranean deity; and cannellini beans from Abruzzo, small, shining pearls of flavor. There are also the sweet onions of Boretto, the Roman artichoke, the exquisite fava beans from the Marches—the list could go on. Italian vegetables are destined to become even more diverse and important, as in recent years many people have chosen to follow a vegetarian diet—whether for health, ethical, or environmental reasons—limiting or abolishing consumption of meat and fish (and, in some cases, also of dairy products).

Within an Italian-style meal, vegetables are utilized not only in the preparation of various courses in the menu, but as the protagonists of side dishes that accompany the meat- or fish-based main course. They can be enjoyed raw or cooked: steamed, stewed, sautéed, baked au gratin, marinated, fried, prepared as *trifolati* (thinly sliced and sautéed with garlic, olive oil, and parsley) or grilled.

The concept of the side dish is relatively recent—within the past couple of centuries. Yet in ancient Rome, for example—according to the poet Petronius in his *Satyricon*—rolled fig leaves stuffed with a mixture of cooked vegetables and mashed legumes were served at the tables of the wealthy. It may be possible, however, that these played the role of main courses, rather than serving as escorts to "heartier" dishes.

If carefully chosen, any side dish can enhance the flavor of a course, but it can also be a delicious dish on its own, especially if the vegetables are "reinforced" by the presence of a protein such as cheese or eggs, as in the tasty Eggplant Parmigiano, or the Leek Flan with Taleggio Cheese Fondue. Side dishes can also play a solo role, even those consisting solely of legumes, such as Italian White Beans with Sage. When legumes are combined with grains, such as those offered in a slice of bread, a high-quality protein is created (comparable to animal products), allowing the side to become a main dish. Naturally, if the side dish is presented as such, the serving size should be smaller, in order to maintain a harmony of proportion with the main dish it accompanies. If, instead, it is to assume the dignity of a main dish, the amount served may be increased.

To create a more convivial spirit—that cozy atmosphere of conversation, laughter, gestures, and exuberance so typically Italian—the side dish should not be served in individual portions but in a single serving dish that can then be passed from one diner to the next. And for it to work perfectly, it ought to follow a few rules. First, select the side dish either for affinity or for contrast, but never for homogeneity, so that the side dish finds its position "in front of" or "beside" the course. Then, where possible, it ought to provide variety, with from three to eight ingredients. Finally, it should be prepared with seasonal ingredients, found as locally as possible.

For this volume, the Academia Barilla, an international center dedicated to the preservation and promotion of Italian cuisine, has selected 40 of the best side dishes from the Italian cooking tradition. They encompass a wealth of colors, textures and aromas; the utmost respect for the high quality of primary ingredients; the simplicity of preparation that itself creates elegance; and, above all, the pleasure of sharing.

Some side dishes are frequently prepared as accompaniments to particular main courses. For example, mashed potatoes are traditionally served in Italy with cooked pork sausages, like *cotechino* or *zampone* (pig's trotter). Even so, this delicate side can be combined equally as well with other meat dishes, or with whatever your intuition suggests, from fried fish to a cheese platter (preferably a tasty selection with intense flavor). Another good example is *lampascioni* (tassel hyacinth), with its bulbs resembling small onions but with a slightly bitter taste, and typical of the cuisine of Puglia and Basilicata. They are frequently combined with meat dishes, but nothing prevents their being served with an array of main courses. Vegetables that are best suited to being breaded or fried in batter, like artichokes or cauliflower, are ideal with white meats or white fish, and they also do quite nicely beside a creamy ricotta. And while a salad of raw vegetables is excellent with fresh summer dishes such as a carpaccio of meat or a fish, it can also lighten up a succulent roast or an appetizing dish of mixed fried seafood.

ASPARAGUS WITH EGG SAUCE

Preparation time: 15 minutes Cooking time: 8 minutes Difficulty: easy

4 SERVINGS

2 1/4 lbs. (1 kg) **asparagus**
3 large **eggs**, *hard-cooked*
2 **anchovies**, *rinsed, filleted and chopped*
1 tbsp. **capers**, *chopped*
Juice of 1 **lemon**
1/2 cup (100 ml) **extra-virgin olive oil**
Salt and pepper *to taste*

Clean the asparagus, tie it in bunches and stand upright in a tall, narrow pot.
Add cold water until 2/3 of the stalks are covered and simmer
for about 8 minutes.
Halve the hard-cooked eggs and separate the yolks from the whites. Press the
egg yolks through a sieve into a bowl, add 2 tablespoons lemon juice and
very slowly, stirring continuously, pour in as much olive oil as necessary
to achieve a thin sauce.
Chop the egg whites and add half to the sauce (reserving the other half for
garnish). Add the capers and anchovies, season with salt and pepper and add
lemon juice to taste. Pour the sauce in a shallow bowl, then arrange the
asparagus, hot or cold, on top. Garnish with the remaining egg whites.

ARTICHOKES ALLA CAVOUR

Preparation time: 20 minutes   Cooking time: 10 minutes   Difficulty: easy

4 SERVINGS

8 **baby artichokes**
2 large **eggs**, hard-cooked
1 **sprig of parsley**
Juice of 1 **lemon**
2 **anchovies**, rinsed and filleted
1/2 stick **unsalted butter**
Parmigiano-Reggiano cheese, grated (as needed)

Heat the oven to 400°F (200°C). Clean artichokes by slicing at least 1/4 inch (1/2 cm) off the tops and bottoms and removing the tough outer leaves at the bottom. Boil the artichokes in a pot of salted water and lemon juice for about 15 minutes; drain.
Melt 1 tablespoon of butter. Drizzle the artichokes with the melted butter and roll them in Parmigiano-Reggiano. Place them in a baking dish and bake for a few minutes, or until cheese is golden brown.
Finely chop the eggs with 1 tbsp. parsley leaves and the anchovies. Melt remaining 3 tablespoons of butter in a small saucepan and heat until it is foaming, then blend in the egg-anchovy-parsley mixture. Stir well and pour over the artichokes. Serve hot.

ROMAN JEWISH-STYLE ARTICHOKES

Preparation time: 20 minutes Cooking time: 25 minutes Difficulty: easy

4 SERVINGS

4 *globe artichokes*
Juice of 1 lemon
Extra-virgin olive oil, as needed
Salt and pepper to taste

Clean artichokes by slicing at least 1/4 inch (0.5 cm) off the tops. Cut the stems, leaving about 1 inch (3 cm). With a very sharp knife, cut off the top third of the leaves. Soak the artichokes in water with lemon juice in a nonreactive bowl so they do not turn black.

Meanwhile, pour olive oil in a pot or skillet, enough to immerse the artichokes, and heat to 270°F (130°C) on a deep-fry thermometer. Drain the artichokes of excess water; pat dry with a clean kitchen towel. Knock the leafy parts of the artichokes together to help open the leaves. Flatten them lightly on a chopping board and spread the leaves out gently (as in photo). Sprinkle a pinch of salt and pepper inside the leaves. Fry the artichokes for about 20 minutes, or until a knife can easily pierce the flesh. Transfer to paper towels to drain. When it is time to serve them, put them back in the hot oil at 350°F (175°C) for 3 to 5 minutes, until crunchy. Transfer to paper towels to drain, then serve hot.

STIR-FRIED BROCCOLI RABE

Preparation time: 15 minutes Cooking time: 10 minutes Difficulty: easy

4 SERVINGS

3 1/3 lbs. (1 1/2 kg) **broccoli rabe,** *chopped*
3 1/2 tbsp. (50 ml) **extra-virgin olive oil**
2 cloves **garlic,** *thinly sliced*
Crushed red pepper *to taste*
Salt *to taste*

Heat the olive oil with the garlic and the crushed pepper in a skillet until the garlic is golden but not browned. Add the broccoli rabe. Season with salt and cook for 10 minutes over medium heat, stirring frequently.

STUFFED ONIONS

Preparation time: 30 minutes Cooking time: 40 minutes Difficulty: easy

4 SERVINGS

3 1/3 lbs. (1 1/2 kg) **small onions** *(such as borettane or cipollini)*
1 bunch **fresh herbs** *(such as parsley, sage, rosemary, thyme, basil and mint)*
7 tbsp. (100 g) **unsalted butter**, *plus more for topping*
7 oz. (200 g) **fresh breadcrumbs** *(about 1 3/4 cups plus 1 tbsp.)*
1/2 cup (100 ml) **milk**
1 oz. (30 g) **raisins** *(3 tablespoons)*
4 large **eggs**
7 oz. (200 g) **Parmigiano-Reggiano cheese**, *grated (about 2 cups)*
Salt *to taste*

Heat the oven to 350°F (180°C). Remove the outer layer of the onions, then boil them, cut them horizontally and scoop out the centers. Finely chop the centers from the boiled onions together with the herbs. Melt the butter in a saucepan and sauté the onion-herb mixture; season with salt.

Meanwhile, soak the breadcrumbs in the milk and soften the raisins in warm water. In a bowl, mix the herb-onion mixture with the breadcrumbs, the raisins, 2 eggs and 1/2 cup Parmigiano-Reggiano until combined.

Stuff the boiled onions with the mixture and arrange the onions in a baking dish. Beat the remaining 2 eggs with the remaining 1 1/2 cups Parmigiano-Reggiano, adding a little milk. Pour the mixture over the onions, almost covering them. Top each onion with a piece of butter and bake until the surface is golden brown.

MARSALA-GLAZED PEARL ONIONS

Preparation time: 15 minutes Cooking time: 20 minutes Difficulty: easy

4 SERVINGS

1 3/4 lbs. (800 g) **pearl onions**, *such as borettane or cipollini*
3 tbsp. (40 g) **unsalted butter**
3 tbsp. (40 g) **sugar**
1/3 cup plus 1 1/2 tbsp. (100 ml) **dry Marsala wine**
1 cup (250 ml) **beef broth**
Salt *to taste*

Trim and peel the onions, then heat in a pan with the butter and sugar. When the sugar is completely dissolved, add the Marsala wine, continuing to cook until it has evaporated. Slowly pour in the broth, cover and continue to cook over low heat until onions are tender, about 15 minutes. When cooking is nearly complete, remove the cover and reduce the cooking sauce to the desired thickness.

CONDIGLIONE

Preparation time: 20 minutes Difficulty: easy

4 SERVINGS

1 1/3 lbs. (600 g) **tomatoes** *(not too ripe), cut into wedges*
7 oz. (200 g) **bell peppers**, *thinly sliced*
7 oz. (200 g) **cucumbers**, *peeled and sliced into rounds*
5 oz. (150 g) **red onions**, *thinly sliced*
1 1/2 oz. (40 g) **salted anchovies**, *rinsed, filleted and halved*
1 3/4 oz. (50 g) **black olives** *(preferably from Liguria)*
5 **fresh basil leaves**, *torn; plus more for garnish*
1 tbsp. (15 ml) **white wine vinegar**
3 1/2 tbsp. (50 ml) **extra-virgin olive oil** *(preferably from Liguria)*
1 clove **garlic**
Salt *to taste*

Place all the vegetables in a large salad bowl and add the olives, anchovies, basil and whole clove garlic (or thinly sliced for a more intense flavor). Dress the salad with oil and vinegar and season with salt. Let salad marinate for about 10 minutes, remove the garlic, if desired, and serve. Alternatively, arrange the cucumbers in a circle on a large serving plate, overlapping them slightly, and mound the salad in the center. Garnish with a basil leaf.

ITALIAN WHITE BEANS
WITH SAGE

Preparation time: 1 hour 20 minutes Soaking: 12 hours
Cooking time: 1 hour 20 minutes Difficulty: easy

4 SERVINGS

14 oz. (400 g) **dried toscanelli** *or cannellini beans*
14 oz. (400 g) **ripe tomatoes**
3 1/2 tbsp. (50 ml) **extra-virgin olive oil**
2 cloves **garlic**, *chopped*
1 **sprig sage**
Salt and pepper *to taste*

Soak the beans in cold water overnight; drain. Transfer beans to a pot with
enough cold unsalted water to cover them. Bring to a boil and cook until beans
are tender, about 1 hour.

Meanwhile, in another pot of boiling water, blanch the tomatoes for 10 to 15
seconds, then peel them, remove the seeds and dice. Heat the oil in a skillet and
add the garlic. Add the tomatoes and sauté for 10 minutes. Add the cooked
beans, season with salt and pepper and cook for another 10 minutes. Garnish
with the whole or chopped sage, as desired.

FAVA BEANS
WITH ANCHOVIES

Preparation time: 10 minutes Cooking time: 5 minutes Difficulty: easy

4 SERVINGS

2 1/4 lbs. (1 kg) **fresh fava beans**
2 cloves **garlic**, *chopped*
Pinch of **marjoram**
4 **anchovies**, *rinsed, filleted and chopped (optional)*
4 tbsp. (60 ml) **extra-virgin olive oil**
Vinegar *to taste*
Salt and pepper *to taste*

Shell the fava beans. Bring a pot of salted water to a boil and cook the fava beans until *al dente*, about 5 minutes, then drain.
Meanwhile, prepare the sauce: Mix the garlic, marjoram, vinegar, olive oil and anchovies, if desired. Season with salt and pepper and serve with fava beans. Alternatively, serve the fava beans with chopped fresh chives, oil and salt and pepper to taste.

BAKED FENNEL

Preparation time: 10 minutes Cooking time: 20 minutes Difficulty: easy

4 SERVINGS

14 oz. (400 g) **fennel bulbs**
3 1/2 oz. (100 g) **Parmigiano-Reggiano cheese**, *grated (about 1 cup)*
3 1/2 tbsp. (50 g) **unsalted butter**
Salt *to taste*

Heat the oven to 375°F (190°C). Bring a pot of salted water to a boil. Rinse the fennel bulbs, cook until crisp-tender, then drain. Once cooled, cut into thick slices.
Butter a 9-inch baking dish.
Melt the remaining butter in a saucepan.
In the baking dish, arrange a layer of fennel, then sprinkle with some of the Parmigiano-Reggiano and drizzle with some melted butter. Add a second layer of fennel, cheese and melted butter, repeating until all the ingredients are used.
Bake the fennel until the top is browned, about 10 minutes.

POTATO FRITTERS

Preparation time: 40 minutes Cooking time: 30 minutes Difficulty: medium

4 SERVINGS

1 1/2 lbs. (700 g) **potatoes**
3 1/2 oz. (100 g) **Parmigiano-Reggiano cheese**, *grated (about 1 cup)*
1/3 cup plus 1 1/2 tbsp. (100 ml) **water**
3 1/2 tbsp. (50 g) **unsalted butter**, *cut into pieces*
1/2 cup (60 g) **all-purpose flour**, *sifted*
2 large **eggs**
Salt *to taste*
Nutmeg *to taste*
Vegetable oil, *for frying*

Wash the potatoes and boil them, skins on, in a pot of lightly salted water until tender, about 15 minutes.

Peel potatoes, then mash them in a bowl (preferably with a potato ricer). Add the Parmigiano-Reggiano and some grated nutmeg.

Meanwhile, bring the 1/3 cup plus 1 1/2 tablespoons of water, the butter and a pinch of salt to a boil in a saucepan. Add the flour and stir to combine, using a wooden spatula, until the dough comes away from the sides of the saucepan.

Remove from heat and let cool, then stir in the eggs, one at a time.

In a large pot, heat oil until shimmering. Meanwhile, combine the potato and flour mixtures and season with salt, if desired. Using a pastry bag, form rings of dough on buttered parchment paper. In batches, fry the potato fritters in the oil until golden. Using a slotted spoon, transfer to paper towels to drain. Sprinkle them with salt. Alternatively, you can form the fritters using two tablespoons, carefully dropping the dough balls directly into the oil.

BATTER-FRIED
MIXED VEGETABLES

Preparation time: 30 minutes Cooking time: 5 minutes Difficulty: easy

4 SERVINGS

5 oz. (150 g) **zucchini**, cut into matchsticks
5 oz. (150 g) **bell peppers**, cut into matchsticks
5 oz. (150 g) **eggplant**, cut into matchsticks
5 oz. (150 g) **red onions** (preferably Tropea), cut into matchsticks
1 3/4 oz. (50 g) **squash blossoms**
3/4 cup plus 1 1/2 tbsp. (200 ml) **milk**
1 1/2 cups (200 g) **all-purpose flour**
Extra-virgin olive oil, for frying
Salt to taste

Heat oil in a large pot until hot and shimmering. Dip all the vegetables and the whole squash blossoms in the milk. Dredge them in the flour, shaking off any excess, and fry them in the oil until golden brown. Using a slotted spoon, transfer them to paper towels to drain. Sprinkle them with salt and serve hot.

FRIED MUSHROOMS

Preparation time: 20 minutes   Cooking time: 5–6 minutes   Difficulty: easy

4 SERVINGS

1 lb. (500 g) **mushrooms**, *such as porcini or button mushrooms*
1 1/2 tbsp. (25 ml) **extra-virgin olive oil**
1 clove **garlic**, *chopped*
1 tbsp. **chopped fresh parsley**
Salt and pepper *to taste*

Clean the mushrooms thoroughly, removing the soil and wiping them with a damp cloth. Cut them into 1/12-inch-thick slices. Heat the olive oil in a skillet and sauté the garlic. Add the mushrooms and parsley and sauté them for 2 to 4 minutes. Season with salt and pepper.

CANNELLINI BEAN STEW

Preparation time: 15 minutes Soaking: overnight
Cooking time: 40 minutes Difficulty: easy

4 SERVINGS

7 oz. (200 g) **cannellini beans**
7 oz. (200 g) **tomatoes**, *peeled, seeded and diced*
2 tbsp. (30 ml) **extra-virgin olive oil**
1 clove **garlic**, *chopped*
1 tbsp. **chopped fresh parsley**
1 **sprig thyme**
Salt and pepper *to taste*

Soak the cannellini beans in cold water overnight; drain.
Boil in a pot of unsalted water for 1 hour.
Heat the olive oil in a pan, add the parsley, garlic and whole sprig of thyme.
Drain the cooked cannellini beans just a little, then add the beans and the
tomatoes. Season with a pinch of salt and pepper and continue cooking for a
few more minutes. Serve with additional pepper.

BEET SALAD

Preparation time: 10 minutes Marinating time: 15 minutes Difficulty: easy

4 SERVINGS

1 1/3 lbs. (600 g) **beets**
7 oz. (200 g) **mixed salad greens**
1 packed cup (75 g) **slivered almonds**
1/2 cup (75 g) **chopped pistachios**
1/4 cup (60 ml) **extra-virgin olive oil**
1 tbsp. plus 1 tsp. (20 ml) **white wine vinegar**
1 clove **garlic**
Salt and pepper *to taste*

Heat the oven to 400°F (200°C). Wrap the beets in aluminum foil and bake until you can easily pierce them with a fork, about 1 hour. When the beets are cool enough to handle, peel and dice them. Mix beets together in a bowl with the olive oil, vinegar, salt, pepper and garlic. Allow to marinate for at least 15 minutes and then remove the garlic. Arrange the salad greens on plates and top with beets. Garnish with almonds and pistachios and serve.

CAULIFLOWER SALAD

Preparation time: 10 minutes Cooking time: 5 minutes Difficulty: easy

4 SERVINGS

1 **head cauliflower**, *divided into florets*
12 **pitted black olives**
1 tbsp. **capers**, *rinsed*
1 **pickled bell pepper**, *drained and thinly sliced*
2 **anchovies**, *rinsed, filleted and finely chopped*
1 tbsp. **vinegar**
2 tbsp. (30 ml) **extra-virgin olive oil**
Salt *to taste*

Boil the cauliflower in a pot of salted water until *al dente*, about 5 minutes.
Dress the cauliflower with the olive oil and vinegar and combine with the olives,
capers, anchovies and bell pepper. Toss salad gently, season with salt,
if desired, and serve.

LAMPASCIONI SALAD

Preparation time: 15 minutes Soaking: 24 hours
Cooking time: 40 minutes Difficulty: easy

4 SERVINGS

1 lb. 1 5/8 oz. (500 g) **lampascioni** *(Muscari comosum, or grape hyacinth bulbs,
also known as wild onions; available at Italian specialty-foods stores and online)*
3 tbsp. (40 ml) **extra-virgin olive oil**
4 tsp. (20 ml) **white wine vinegar**
2 **sprigs parsley** *(1 chopped;1 reserved for garnish)*
Salt and pepper *to taste*

Clean the *lampascioni* by removing the outer leaves, rinse well and soak in cold
water for 24 hours, changing the water often. Bring a pot of unsalted water to a
boil and cook *lampascioni* over low heat for about 40 minutes, or until tender.
Let cool in the cooking liquid. Drain and season with salt and pepper. Dress with
vinegar, olive oil and parsley. Mix well and serve. Garnish with parsley.

MANGO SALAD
WITH YELLOW PEPPERS AND CARROTS

Preparation time: 20 minutes Difficulty: easy

4 SERVINGS

1 1/3 lbs. (600 g) **mango**, *peeled and cut into matchsticks*
7 oz. (200 g) **carrots**, *peeled and cut into matchsticks*
8 oz. (250 g) **yellow bell pepper**, *thinly sliced*
1/3 cup plus 1 1/2 tbsp. (100 ml) **extra-virgin olive oil**
Juice of 1 **lemon**
Salt *to taste*

In a blender, purée one-quarter of the mango with salt, lemon juice and the olive oil. Combine the remaining mango, the carrots and the bell pepper and drizzle with the dressing. Serve on plates or in halved, seeded bell peppers.

CHRISTMAS SALAD

Preparation time: 25 minutes Difficulty: easy

4 SERVINGS

11 oz. (300 g) **sweet chicory** *(outer ribs discarded), chopped*
11 oz. (300 g) **celery**
2 tbsp. **capers,** *rinsed*
2 tbsp. **green olives,** *chopped*
1 **orange**
1 **lemon**
Seeds from 1 **pomegranate**
2 tbsp. (30 ml) **extra-virgin olive oil**
Salt *to taste*

Boil the chicory and celery separately, uncovered, for about 5 minutes.
Drain and let cool.
Combine with olive oil, capers and olives. Mix well and arrange on a serving dish. Remove peel and pith from orange and lemon. Use a paring knife to slice between the sections and membranes of each fruit; remove the segments whole and place on top of the salad. Garnish with pomegranate seeds.

PEAR SALAD
WITH PARMIGIANO-REGGIANO

Preparation time: 20 minutes Difficulty: easy

4 SERVINGS

3 1/2 oz. (100 g) **Parmigiano-Reggiano cheese**, *shaved*
3 **pears**
1 **head lettuce**, *cut into large pieces*
10 **pitted black olives**
1 **bell pepper**, *thinly sliced*
30 **walnuts**, *coarsely chopped*
Juice of 1 **lemon**
6 tbsp. (80 ml) **extra-virgin olive oil**
Salt and pepper *to taste*

Peel and dice 2 pears. Slice remaining pear and set aside for garnish. Squeeze the lemon juice into a mixing bowl and add salt to taste, letting salt dissolve; then add the olive oil and pepper to taste. Whisk until emulsified. Combine the vegetables, walnuts, olives, diced pears and Parmigiano-Reggiano in a salad bowl. Drizzle with the dressing and toss well. Garnish with pear slices and serve.

PEAR SALAD
WITH GORGONZOLA AND WALNUTS

Preparation time: 15 minutes Difficulty: easy

4 SERVINGS

2 **pears**
1/4 lb. (120 g) **Gorgonzola cheese**
7 oz. (200 g) **red or green leaf lettuce**
1 3/4 oz. (50 g) **walnuts**
1/3 cup plus 1 1/2 tbsp. (100 ml) **extra-virgin olive oil**
Salt and pepper *to taste*

Halve the pears, scoop out the flesh (to create bowls) and dice the pear flesh. Mix the diced pears with the Gorgonzola and fill the pear halves with the mixture. On salad plates, arrange the lettuce leaves and set one pear half on top of each salad. Sprinkle with the walnuts, season with salt and pepper and drizzle with olive oil.

Alternatively, dice the pears, leaving the skin on if you wish. On plates, arrange the salad leaves, then top with the pears, crumbled Gorgonzola chunks, walnuts. Season with salt and pepper, and drizzle with olive oil.

ARUGULA SALAD
WITH PARMIGIANO-REGGIANO

Preparation time: 15 minutes Difficulty: easy

4 SERVINGS

7 oz. (200 g) **arugula**
5 oz. (150 g) **Parmigiano-Reggiano cheese**
3 1/2 tbsp. (50 ml) **extra-virgin olive oil**
1 tbsp. (15 ml) **balsamic vinegar**
Salt and pepper *to taste*

Rinse and dry the arugula. Whisk the balsamic vinegar, olive oil and salt and
pepper to taste in a small bowl. Thinly slice the Parmigiano-Reggiano with a
mandoline or vegetable peeler. On salad plates, arrange the arugula and
sprinkle with the Parmigiano-Reggiano.
Drizzle with the dressing.

GRILLED POTATO STACKS

Preparation time: 30 minutes Difficulty: easy

4–6 SERVINGS

1 1/3 lbs. (600 g) **potatoes** *(a mix of yellow, white and purple)*
3 1/2 tbsp. (50 ml) **extra-virgin olive oil**
7 oz. (200 g) **tomatoes**, *diced*
Sprigs of thyme
Salt and pepper *to taste*

Scrub the potatoes and boil them, skins on, in a pot of salted water until cooked but still firm, 12 to 15 minutes. Let cool, then peel and cut them into 1/4-inch-thick slices. Transfer to a very hot grill or griddle greased with oil and cook the slices for a few minutes. Season with salt, pepper, a drizzle of olive oil and a few sprigs of thyme. Assemble the stacks by layering the potato slices in a baking pan. Garnish with the tomatoes and sprigs of thyme.

EGGPLANT PARMIGIANA

Preparation time: 1 1/2 hours Cooking time: 30 minutes Difficulty: easy

4 SERVINGS

1 1/3 lbs. (600 g) **eggplant**, *thinly sliced lengthwise*
1/3 cup plus 1 tbsp. (50 g) **all-purpose flour**
1 1/4 cups (300 g) **ready-made tomato sauce**
2 large **eggs**, *lightly beaten*
5 oz. (150 g) **mozzarella**, *thinly sliced*
3 1/2 oz. (100 g) **Parmigiano-Reggiano cheese**, *grated (about 1 cup)*
Olive oil, *for frying*
Fresh basil, *torn*
Salt *to taste*

Put the eggplant slices in a colander, salt lightly and allow to drain for about 30 minutes. Heat an oven to 375°F (190°C). Heat olive oil in a large pot until shimmering. Dredge the eggplant in the flour, shaking off any excess, then dip in the eggs. In batches, fry the eggplant in the oil until golden. Using a slotted spoon, transfer to paper towels to drain. Sprinkle them with salt.

Spoon a thin layer of tomato sauce into the bottom of a 9- by 13-inch baking dish, then arrange a layer of fried eggplant and then a layer of mozzarella. Cover with a layer of tomato sauce, flavored with a little basil. Sprinkle with a handful of Parmigiano-Reggiano and repeat the process, starting with another layer of fried eggplant and proceeding in the same order. Continue until you have used all the ingredients, finishing with a layer of eggplant. Cover the top layer of eggplant with tomato sauce and a sprinkling of Parmigiano-Reggiano. Bake until golden, about 30 minutes. Let rest for at least 20 minutes before serving.

FRIED POTATOES

Preparation time: 20 minutes Cooking time: 5-7 minutes Difficulty: easy

4 SERVINGS

1 lb. (400 g) **yellow potatoes**, *such as Yukon Gold*
Oil, *for frying*
Salt *to taste*

Peel potatoes and soak in a bowl of cold water, changing water several times. For "Paris-style" potatoes, scoop out rounds using a special corer with a diameter of 1 inch (2 1/2 cm). For "potato chips," slice very thin using a mandoline. For French fries, cut into regular slices of about 1/4 inch (7 mm), then into matchsticks the same size. For waffle fries, use a ripple-cut blade, rotating the potato by 90 degrees between one cut and the next. For matchstick potatoes, cut into slices of about 1/10 inch (2 mm), then into matchsticks of the same size. For each of the cuts (except the chips, and matchsticks): Drain potatoes and dry them.

Heat the oil in a large pot until it reaches 300°F (150°C) on a deep-fry thermometer. Fry each cut separately for about 5 minutes or until cooked, but not until darkened. Using a slotted spoon, transfer to paper towels to drain. Increase the temperature of the oil to 350°F (180°C). Immerse the partially cooked potatoes again and fry until golden. Transfer to paper towels to drain again and sprinkle with salt. For the chips and matchsticks, there is no need for precooking; proceed directly to frying at 350°F (180°C).

POTATOES STUFFED
WITH GOAT CHEESE

Preparation time: 30 minutes Cooking time: 40 minutes Difficulty: easy

4 SERVINGS

4 medium **potatoes**
5 oz. (150 g) **fresh goat cheese**
Salt and pepper *to taste*

Heat the oven to 350°F (180°C). Scrub the potatoes, leaving their skins on. Wrap them individually in aluminum foil and bake in the oven for about 30 minutes. Cut them in half, season with a pinch of salt and top each with 1 tablespoon goat cheese and a sprinkling of pepper.

PEPERONATA

Preparation time: 15 minutes   Cooking time: 30 minutes   Difficulty: easy

4 SERVINGS

1 lb. (500 g) **peppers** *(preferably a mixture of yellow, red and orange)*
3 1/2 oz. (100 g) **onion**, *sliced*
1/3 oz. (10 g) **capers**
2 **salt-packed anchovies**, *rinsed and filleted*
1 clove **garlic**
3 1/2 tbsp. (50 ml) **extra-virgin olive oil**
Salt and pepper *to taste*

Heat the oil in a pan and sauté the onion, garlic, capers and anchovies. Rinse the peppers, trim, remove the seeds, cut into large pieces and add to the pan. Season the mixture with salt and pepper and cook for about 20 minutes.

SICILIAN-STYLE STUFFED PEPPERS

Preparation time: 30 minutes Cooking time: 25 minutes Difficulty: easy

4 SERVINGS

4 **peppers** *(yellow and orange)*
8 1/2 oz. (240 g) **breadcrumbs**
4 **tomatoes**
4 **salted anchovies**, *rinsed, filleted and chopped*
2 tbsp. **capers**
1 3/4 oz. (50 g) **Caciocavallo cheese or provolone**, *grated (about 1/2 cup)*
Extra-virgin olive oil, *as needed*
Fresh basil
Salt and pepper *to taste*

Heat the oven to 400°F (200°C). Using the tip of a knife, remove the stalk and the seeds of the peppers, taking care not to break them. Cut them in half. Brown the breadcrumbs lightly in a nonstick pan and season with salt, pepper and basil. Add the cheese, capers, tomatoes and anchovies. Mix well, adding a little oil, and stuff the peppers with the mixture.
Place the peppers in a greased baking dish, add a little oil, cover with aluminum foil and bake for 15 minutes. Remove the aluminum foil and cook for another 10 minutes, drizzling with more oil, if necessary. Serve warm or at room temperature.

STIR-FRIED ROMAN CHICORY
WITH ANCHOVY SAUCE

Preparation time: 15 minutes Cooking time: 10 minutes Difficulty: easy

4 SERVINGS

3 1/3 **puntarelle** (Catalogna frastagliata *chicory shoots, leaves discarded), chopped*
3 1/2 tbsp. (50 ml) **extra-virgin olive oil**
2 **salt-packed anchovies**, *rinsed and filleted*
2 cloves **garlic**, *thinly sliced*
1 **red chile pepper**, *chopped*
Salt *to taste*

Heat the olive oil in a skillet and sauté the garlic, anchovies and red pepper. Do not let the garlic brown too much but cook the mixture until the anchovies break into pieces. Add the puntarelle, season with salt and cook for 10 minutes over medium heat, stirring frequently.

MASHED POTATOES

Preparation time: 20 minutes Difficulty: easy

4–6 SERVINGS

CLASSIC
*1 lb. (500 g) **potatoes**, peeled*
*1 1/2 cups (350 ml) **milk***
*5 1/2 tbsp. (80 g) **butter***
*3 1/2 oz. (100 g) **Parmigiano-Reggiano***
***cheese**, grated (about 1 cup)*
***Nutmeg** to taste*
***Salt** to taste*

WITH CARROTS
*1/2 lb. (250 g) **potatoes**, peeled*
*1 lb. (500 g) **carrots***
*3/4 cup (180 ml) **milk***
*2 tbsp. (30 g) **butter***

*2 1/2 oz. (70 g) **Parmigiano-Reggiano***
***cheese**, grated (about 1/3 cup)*
***Nutmeg** to taste*
***Salt** to taste*

WITH PEAS
*7 oz. (200 g) **potatoes**, peeled*
*1 lb. (500 g) **peas***
*2/3 cups (150 ml) **milk***
*2 tbsp. (30 g) **butter***
*1 3/4 oz. (50 g) **Parmigiano-Reggiano***
***cheese**, grated (about 1/2 cup)*
***Nutmeg** to taste*
***Salt** to taste*

Boil the potatoes in a pot of lightly salted water for about 25 minutes, or until a small knife can easily pierce a potato. For the flavored mashed potatoes, cook the other vegetables together with the potatoes. Then drain and pass the vegetables through a food mill or a potato ricer and put them in a pot. Combine the butter, the Parmigiano-Reggiano and some nutmeg. In a separate saucepan, heat the milk to just below boiling and add to the mashed potatoes. Season with salt, mix thoroughly and serve.

RATATOUILLE

Preparation time: 10 minutes Cooking time: 20 minutes Difficulty: easy

4 SERVINGS

7 oz. (200 g) **eggplant**, *in 3/4-inch dice*
11 oz. (300 g) **zucchini**, *in 3/4-inch dice*
7 oz. (200 g) **grape tomatoes**, *halved*
6 oz. (180 g) **red onion**, *thinly sliced*
3 1/2 oz. (100 g) **red bell peppers**, *cut into 3/4-inch cubes*
3 1/2 oz. (100 g) **yellow bell peppers**, *in 3/4-inch dice*
1 clove **garlic**
4 **fresh basil leaves**, *torn*
1/3 cup plus 1 1/2 tbsp. (100 ml) **extra-virgin olive oil**
Salt and pepper *to taste*

Heat the olive oil in a pan over medium heat, add the garlic and the onion and fry until softened. Add the peppers and cook for 3 minutes. Add the eggplant and the zucchini. Fry for a few minutes, then add the tomatoes and season with salt and pepper. Lower heat, add basil and continue to cook.

RÖSTI

Preparation time: 10 minutes Cooking time: 15 minutes Difficulty: easy

4 SERVINGS

1 3/4 lbs. (750 g) **potatoes**, *peeled*
3 1/2 tbsp. (50 g) **unsalted butter**
Salt and pepper *to taste*

Grate the potatoes using the large-hole side of a box grater or cut them into thin matchsticks using a julienne attachment on a mandoline or food processor. Melt the butter in a nonstick skillet and add the potatoes. Season with salt and pepper and stir using two spatulas. When the potatoes begin to soften, flatten them using the spatulas, shaping them into pancake form. Continue to cook until the crust is golden, then turn over as one piece, and brown the other side.

CABBAGE SOUFFLÉ

Preparation time: 40 minutes Cooking time: 40 minutes Difficulty: medium

4 SERVINGS

1/2 **Savoy cabbage**, *shredded*
1 **onion**, *thinly sliced*
1 **bay leaf**
4 large **eggs** *plus 3 large egg yolks*
7 oz. (200 ml) **heavy cream**
Small bunch of **fresh basil**
1 3/4 lbs. (800 g) **Fontina cheese**, *diced*
Milk, *as needed*
Salt and pepper *to taste*

Heat the oven to 300°F (150°C).
Stew the onion and cabbage together with the bay leaf. Remove the bay leaf, add the basil and pulse in a blender. Strain through a conical strainer, add the whole eggs and the cream and whisk well. Butter 4 ramekins, pour in the mixture and place, covered, in a large baking pan of hot water, so that water reaches halfway up ramekins. Bake in oven until firm.
Place the Fontina in a baking dish, cover with milk, add a pinch of pepper and cook in the hot-water bath, mixing with a wooden spoon until a smooth mixture is achieved. Add the yolks, one at a time, to the Fontina cream, taking care to blend them in without cooking them. Pour the Fontina sauce over the soufflés, or put a thin layer of sauce on each plate and place the soufflés on the sauce.

BAKED RED CABBAGE

Preparation time: 30 minutes   Cooking time: 30 minutes   Difficulty: medium

4 SERVINGS

14 oz. (400 g) **red cabbage**
2 tbsp. (30 ml) **heavy cream**
3 1/2 tbsp. (50 ml) **extra-virgin olive oil**
1 tbsp. plus 2 tsp. (25 ml) **vinegar**
2 tbsp. **finely chopped onion**
7 oz. (200 g) **mixed greens**
1 tbsp. plus 1 tsp. (20 ml) **balsamic vinegar**, *preferably from Modena*
2 large **eggs**
2 oz. (60 g) **Parmigiano-Reggiano cheese**, *grated (about 2/3 cup)*
Mixed fresh herbs *(optional)*
Salt and pepper *to taste*

Heat oven at 325°F (160°C). Blanch the cabbage in boiling salted water with a bit of vinegar. Let it cool, then roughly chop.
Heat the olive oil in a pan and sauté the onion. Add the cabbage and cook for a few minutes; let cool. Mix cabbage mixture with the eggs, cream and Parmigiano-Reggiano. Season with salt and pepper. Transfer the mixture to individual ramekins and place them in a hot-water bath (a large baking pan of hot water filled to reach halfway up ramekins). Bake them for about 30 minutes. Dress the mixed greens with remaining oil, balsamic vinegar and a pinch of salt. Serve them with the baked cabbage and garnish with herbs.

LEEK FLAN
WITH TALEGGIO CHEESE FONDUE

Preparation time: 30 minutes Cooking time: 20 minutes Difficulty: medium

4 SERVINGS

FOR THE FLAN
3/4 lb. (350 g) **leeks**
3 tbsp. (40 g) **unsalted butter**
1 3/4 oz. (50 g) **Parmigiano-Reggiano**
cheese, *grated*
1 cup (250 ml) **heavy cream**
1 1/4 tbsp. (10 g) **all-purpose flour**
2 large **eggs**, *separated*

Salt and pepper *to taste*
Vegetable oil, *for frying*

FOR THE FONDUE
8 3/4 oz. (250 g) **Taleggio cheese**,
diced
2/3 cup (150 ml) **milk**
Salt *to taste*

For the fondue: Bring the milk to a boil in a saucepan, then add the Taleggio. Stir until the Taleggio has melted and the fondue achieves a smooth consistency (if necessary, add more milk). Season with salt.

For the flan: Clean the leeks, cut the white parts into thin strips and rinse them thoroughly; drain and let dry. (Reserve the green leaves for garnish.) Melt the butter in a saucepan, add the leeks (reserving 1 3/4 oz. [50 g] for garnish) and sauté over low heat until soft. Sprinkle with flour, stir well and add the cream. Season with salt and pepper. Bring the mixture to a boil and remove from the heat. Let the mixture cool and then add the egg yolks and the Parmigiano-Reggiano.

Heat the oven to 320°F (160°C). Whip the egg whites until stiff and fold carefully into the leek mixture. Butter ramekins, fill with leek mixture and cook in a hot-water bath in the oven for about 20 minutes.

Meanwhile, heat oil in a pan until shimmering and fry the remaining leeks. Serve the flans with the hot fondue and garnish with the leeks. Use leek greens as decoration.

MARINATED FRIED ZUCCHINI

Preparation time: 30 minutes Marinating: 12 hours Difficulty: easy

4 SERVINGS

1 lb. (500 g) **zucchini** *(2 1/2 medium), cut into small strips*
1/3 cup plus 1 1/2 tbsp. (100 ml) **white wine vinegar**
1/3 cup plus 1 1/2 tbsp. (100 ml) **water**
Bunch of **fresh mint***, chopped*
1 clove **garlic***, thinly sliced*
10 **peppercorns**
Extra-virgin olive oil, *for frying*
Salt *to taste*

Heat oil in a skillet until shimmering. In batches, fry the zucchini until golden brown. Using a slotted spoon, transfer to paper towels to drain. Sprinkle with salt, then place them in a bowl with the mint.

Boil 1/3 cup plus 1 1/2 tablespoons water with the vinegar, peppercorns and garlic for 5 to 6 minutes. (You can alter the water-to-vinegar ratio depending on how much acidity you prefer.) Pour the hot marinade over the zucchini. Let cool, then refrigerate for at least 12 hours. Serve zucchini cold or at room temperature.

ZUCCHINI
WITH RICOTTA CHEESE

Preparation time: 10 minutes Cooking time: 15-20 minutes Difficulty: easy

4 SERVINGS

1 3/4 lbs. (800 g) **zucchini**
10 1/2 oz. (300 g) **ricotta cheese**
1 large **egg**
1 clove **garlic**, *minced*
1 tbsp. **chopped parsley**
3 tbsp. (40 g) **unsalted butter**
Salt *to taste*

Heat the oven to 340°F (170°C). Rinse the zucchini and boil in a pot of salted water. Drain, remove the two ends of the zucchini, cut into halves lengthwise and scoop out the pulp. Pass the ricotta through a fine-mesh sieve, then mix in the egg, garlic and parsley. Fill the zucchini halves with the mixture and arrange in a buttered baking dish. Dot the remaining butter in pieces over the zucchini and bake for 15 to 20 minutes. Serve piping hot.

SWEET-AND-SOUR ZUCCHINI

Preparation time: 15 minutes Cooking time: 15 minutes Difficulty: easy

4 SERVINGS

*2 1/4 lb. (1 kg) small **zucchini***
*1/4 cup (60 ml) **white wine vinegar***
*2 1/8 oz. (60 g) **sugar** (about 1/3 cup)*
***Oil**, for frying*
***Salt** to taste*

To make the sweet-and-sour marinade: In a small frying pan over low heat,
dissolve the sugar in the vinegar and keep warm.
Wash the zucchini and cut into disks 1/4 inch (1/2 cm) thick. Heat oil in a pot until
shimmering. In batches, fry the zucchini. Using a slotted spoon, transfer them to
paper towels to drain. Then arrange them in a baking dish. Sprinkle with
salt and pour the sweet-and-sour marinade over them. (In summer, these are
also good served cold.)

MARINATED ZUCCHINI

Preparation time: 25 minutes Cooking time: 15 minutes
Marinating: 3 hours to overnight Difficulty: easy

4 SERVINGS

1 1/3 lbs. (600 g) **zucchini**, *thinly sliced*
4 large **eggs**
1 clove **garlic**
5 oz. (150 g) **onion**, *thinly sliced*
3 1/2 oz. (100 g) **carrots**, *cut into matchsticks*
3 1/2 oz. (100 g) **celery**, *cut into matchsticks*

Bunch of **fresh sage**
2/3 cup (150 ml) **extra-virgin olive oil**
1 1/4 cups (300 ml) **white wine vinegar**
1 1/4 cups (300 ml) **white wine**
1 1/4 cups (300 ml) **water**
All-purpose flour, *as needed*
Salt *to taste*

Heat 2 tablespoons (30 ml) olive oil in a skillet and sauté the vegetables. Add the garlic, sage, white wine and vinegar and bring to a boil. Add the 1 1/4 cups water and season with salt. Cook for a few minutes and then cover to keep warm while you fry the zucchini.

Meanwhile, beat the eggs in a bowl with a pinch of salt. Dredge the zucchini in the flour, then dip in the beaten eggs and fry in the remaining oil in a skillet. Transfer the zucchini to paper towels to drain. Place the zucchini in a baking dish and cover with the sauce. Let marinate for at least 3 hours or up to overnight.

INGREDIENTS INDEX

PHOTO CREDITS

All photographs are by ACADEMIA BARILLA except the following:
pages 6, 95 ©123RF

. . . .

The Taunton Press
Inspiration for hands-on living®

The Taunton Press, Inc.
63 South Main Street
PO Box 5506, Newtown, CT 06470-5506
e-mail: tp@taunton.com

Translations:
Catherine Howard - Mary Doyle - John Venerella - Free z'be, Paris
Salvatore Ciolfi - Rosetta Translations SARL - Rosetta Translations SARL

LIBRARY OF CONGRESS CATALOGING-IN-PUBLICATION DATA IN PROGRESS
ISBN: 978-1-62710-050-2

Printed in China
10 9 8 7 6 5 4 3 2 1